Taylor Swift

The Essential Trivia Book
143 Questions

13 Fun Facts, 1 Iconic Artist

Olivia James

Contents

Introduction

Are you ready to dive into the enchanting world of Taylor Swift? Get ready to put your knowledge to the test and discover fascinating new facts about the one and only musical sensation who has taken the world by storm!

Welcome to "Taylor Swift: The Essential Trivia Book — 143 Questions, 13 Fun Facts, 1 Iconic Artist"! This is your ultimate, unofficial guide to everything Taylor. It is packed with intriguing trivia, mind-blowing fun facts, and everything in between. Whether you're a die-hard Swiftie or a casual admirer of her music, this book is perfect for anyone who wants to celebrate the incredible journey of this global superstar.

From her humble beginnings as a country sweetheart to her meteoric rise as a pop icon, Taylor Swift has captured the hearts of millions with her unparalleled talent, infectious personality, and unwavering dedication to her craft. Her music has resonated with fans across generations, and her impact on popular culture is undeniable.

In this book, we'll take you on a thrilling journey through Taylor's life, career, and the moments that have defined her as an artist. You'll have the chance to test your Swiftie knowledge with 143 carefully curated trivia questions that cover every aspect of her multifaceted career. From her chart-topping albums, record-breaking tours, iconic fashion moments, and heartfelt lyrics, no stone is left unturned in this comprehensive trivia extravaganza.

But that's not all — we've also included 13 mind-blowing fun facts that will leave you amazed and inspired by Taylor's incredible achievements. Did you know she's the only female artist in history to have six albums sell over 1 million copies in their first week of release? Or that she once caused a 2.3 magnitude earthquake with the sheer power of her live performances? These are just a few of the jaw-dropping facts that await you in this book.

So, are you ready to embark on this exciting adventure? Whether you're a seasoned Swiftie or a new fan eager to learn more, "Taylor Swift: The Essential Trivia Book" takes you into the world of this extraordinary artist. Get ready to sing along, laugh out loud, and be inspired by the one and only Taylor Swift. Let's dive in and celebrate the magic of music together!

CHAPTER 1
Early Life

Hey there, Swifties! Get ready to dive into the incredible story of your favorite superstar, Taylor Swift, and discover where it all began!

We're talking about the one and only Taylor Alison Swift, born on December 13, 1989, in the charming town of West Reading, Pennsylvania. From the moment she entered this world, it was clear that Taylor was destined for greatness. With her loving parents, Scott and Andrea, and her awesome younger brother, Austin, by her side, Taylor grew up on a magical Christmas tree farm, where her love for music and storytelling blossomed.

As a young girl, Taylor's passion for performing shone brighter than the most glittery disco ball. At the tender age of 10, she was already rocking local events and festivals with her incredible voice and undeniable stage presence. And get this—her grandmother, Marjorie, was a professional opera singer! Talk about a family full of talent!

But Taylor's journey to stardom wasn't all sunshine and rainbows. She faced her fair share of challenges and rejections, but did that stop her? No way! With the unwavering support of her family and her own unshakable determination, Taylor chased her dreams all the way to Nashville, the heart of country music.

In between writing heartfelt lyrics and crafting unforgettable melodies, Taylor was just like any other kid. She attended school, made friends, and even had some pretty cool pets, like her beloved Shetland Pony, a few dogs, and two cats.

But there was no denying that music was Taylor's true calling. At 14, she convinced her family to make the big move to Hendersonville, Tennessee, where she could fully immerse herself in the country music scene. And boy, did she make a splash! Taylor was unstoppable, from performing at the legendary Bluebird Café to opening for country music icons like George Strait.

So, there you have it, Swifties—the incredible origin story of your favorite superstar! But hang on tight because we're just getting started. Get ready to dive deeper into Taylor's life with mind-blowing trivia questions, multiple-choice brain-teasers, and jaw-dropping fun facts that will make you feel like you've known her forever!

Think you're the ultimate Taylor Swift fan? Let's see if you can answer these 13 questions about Taylor's early years. Don't worry; the answers are right there waiting for you!

1. What was the name of the Christmas tree farm where Taylor grew up?

2. What was Taylor's "job" on the family's Christmas tree farm?

3. What were the occupations of Taylor's parents, Scott and Andrea Swift?

4. What was the name of the Montessori school Taylor attended for preschool and kindergarten?

5. What was the name of the first song Taylor Swift ever wrote?

6. What was the name of Taylor's Shetland Pony when she was growing up?

7. True or False: Taylor Swift was born on Sunday?

8. In which state was Taylor Swift born?
   a. Tennessee.
   b. Texas.
   c. Pennsylvania.
   d. California.

9. What was the name of Taylor Swift's first single?
   a. "Our Song."
   b. "Love Story."
   c. "Tim McGraw."
   d. "Teardrops on My Guitar."

10. How old was Taylor when she first learned to play the guitar?
    a. 8 years old.
    b. 10 years old.
    c. 12 years old.
    d. 14 years old.

11. Which country music star was Taylor's childhood idol?
    a. Shania Twain.

b. Faith Hill.

c. LeAnn Rimes.

d. Reba McEntire.

12. What was the name of Taylor's first pet, a Shetland pony?

a. Ginger.

b. Butterscotch.

c. Cinnamon.

d. Honey.

13. Which country music star did Taylor open for during her early career?

a. Kenny Chesney.

b. Tim McGraw.

c. George Strait.

d. Brad Paisley.

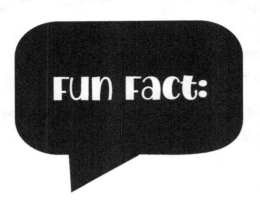

FUN FACT:

Hold on to your glow sticks! Here is a fun and interesting fact about Taylor that will make you love her even more!

Taylor Swift's lucky number is 13! She was born on December 13, 1989, and she's had some incredible moments happen on the 13th of various months throughout her career. For example, her first album went gold in 13 weeks, and her first #1 song had a 13-second intro. Talk about a lucky coincidence!

But it gets even cooler! Taylor loves the number 13 so much that she often incorporates it into her life and music. She's been known to paint the number 13 on her hand before performances for good luck, and she even used to write the number on her arm during her school days.

And get this—when Taylor's first album hit #1 on the Billboard 200 chart, it stayed there for 13 consecutive weeks! It's like the number 13 is her very own lucky charm.

So, whenever you see the number 13, think of your favorite superstar, Taylor Swift, and how this special number has been a magical part of her incredible journey!

CHAPTER 1 ANSWERS

1. Answer: Pine Ridge Farm.

2. Answer: Taylor helped on the Christmas tree farm by picking praying mantis pods off the trees. This was done to ensure the trees were free of pests before being sold.

3. Answer: Scott was a financial advisor, and Andrea was a homemaker and former marketing executive.

4. Answer: Alvernia Montessori School.

5. Answer: "Lucky You."

6. Answer: Ginger.

7. Answer: False. Taylor was born on a Wednesday.

8. Answer: Pennsylvania.

9. Answer: "Tim McGraw."

10. Answer: 12 years old.

11. Answer: LeAnn Rimes.

12. Answer: Ginger.

13. Answer: George Strait.

CHAPTER 2:
Music and Albums

Hey there, Swifties! Are you ready to dive into the magical world of Taylor Swift's music?

From the moment Taylor stepped into the spotlight with her first album back in 2006, it was clear she would be a superstar! With her amazing voice, incredible songwriting skills, and a heart full of stories to share, Taylor has taken us on a wild ride through her music.

Over the years, Taylor has given us eleven incredible albums, each one more amazing than the last! From the country twang of her early songs to the pop perfection of *1989* and the dreamy vibes of *Folklore* and *Evermore* Taylor has tried out so many different sounds and styles. It's like she's always keeping us on our toes, wondering what she'll come up with next!

But what makes Taylor's music so special is how it makes us feel. Every song is like a little piece of her heart, filled with stories about falling in love, dealing with heartbreak, and growing up. It's like she knows exactly what we're going through and puts it into words and music that we can all relate to.

It's no surprise that Taylor's albums have broken so many records and won so many awards. Her music has inspired millions of fans all around the world to pick up a guitar, write their own songs, and chase their dreams. From the teardrops on her guitar to the bad blood between friends, from the love story of "Mine" to the epic tale of "All Too Well," Taylor's songs have become a part of our lives.

But how much do you really know about Taylor's music? Just to give you a quick refresher, here are the amazing albums Taylor has released: *Talor Swift* (2006), *Fearless* (2008), *Speak Now* (2010), *Red* (2012), *1989* (2014), *Reputation* (2017), *Lover* (2019), *Folklore* (2020), *Evermore* (2020), *Fearless (Taylor's Version)* (2021), *Red (Taylor's Version)* (2021), *Midnights* (2022), *Speak Now (Taylor's Version)* (2023), *1989 (Taylor's Version)* (2023), and *The Tortured Poets Department* (2024).

In this chapter, we will put your Swiftie skills to the test with some super fun trivia questions and challenges! We'll explore all the hidden clues in her lyrics, the crazy stories behind her recording sessions, and everything in between. It's like a backstage pass to Taylor's musical world!

Whether you've been a fan since day one or you're just discovering her music now, this chapter is all about celebrating the amazing journey of Taylor Swift and the songs that have stolen our hearts. Test your knowledge and see if you can answer these 13 questions about the one and only Taylor Swift.

1. Which Taylor Swift album features the hit single "Shake It Off"?

2. In which song does Taylor Swift sing about a scarf that smells like her ex-boyfriend?

3. What is the name of the song that Taylor Swift wrote for the movie "The Hunger Games"?

4. In which music video does Taylor Swift play multiple characters, including a nerdy girl and a cheerleader?

5. Which Taylor Swift album is the first album in the history of Spotify to have more than 300 million streams in one day?

6. What is the name of Taylor Swift's third studio album, released in 2010?

7. Which Taylor Swift song became her first number-one single on the Billboard Hot 100?

8. Which of the following albums features the song "Love Story"?
   a. *Speak Now.*
   b. *Fearless.*
   c. *Red.*
   d. *1989.*

9. In which music video does Taylor Swift play a woman who transforms into a zombie?
   a. "Bad Blood."
   b. "Wildest Dreams."
   c. "Out of the Woods."
   d. "Look What You Made Me Do."

10. True or False: The song "The Last Great American Dynasty" is on the *1989* album.

11. Who is the featured artist on Taylor Swift's song "End Game"?

    a. Ed Sheeran and Future.

    b. Kendrick Lamar and Beyoncé.

    c. Drake and Rihanna.

    d. Justin Timberlake and Timbaland.

12. In the music video for "Cardigan," Taylor Swift is seen playing which instrument?

    a. Guitar.

    b. Piano.

    c. Violin.

    d. Harp.

13. In which Taylor Swift song does she mention her cats?

    a. "Gorgeous."

    b. "Shake It Off."

    c. "Blank Space."

    d. "Lover."

FUN FACT:

Hold onto your sequins. Did you know that Taylor Swift's song "All Too Well" was originally super long and over 10 minutes?

When Taylor first wrote the song, it was like a mini-movie that lasted over 10 minutes! Taylor poured her heart out in the lyrics, telling the story of a love that didn't last. But when it was time to put the song on her *Red* album, she had to make it shorter so it would fit.

Even though the song got trimmed down, it still became a huge favorite among Swifties. They loved how honest and emotional the lyrics were and how they could relate to the story Taylor was telling. Years later, Taylor decided to give her fans a special surprise. She re-recorded the *Red* album and included the extra-long version of "All Too Well" that she first wrote. And if you are lucky enough to see the absolutely incredible Eras tour, she has been performing the 10-minute version live!

So, the next time you listen to "All Too Well," remember the amazing journey this song has been on and how much love and hard work Taylor put into creating it. It's a true masterpiece!

CHAPTER 2 ANSWERS

1. Answer: *1989*

2. Answer: "All Too Well."

3. Answer: "Safe & Sound."

4. Answer: "You Belong With Me."

5. Answer: *The Tortured Poets Department.*

6. Answer: *Speak Now.*

7. Answer: "We Are Never Ever Getting Back Together" was Taylor Swift's first number-one single on the Billboard Hot 100, reaching the top spot in 2012.

8. Answer: *Fearless.*

9. Answer: "Look What You Made Me Do."

10. Answer: False; it is on *Folklore.*

11. Answer: Ed Sheeran and Future.

12. Answer: Piano.

13. Answer: "Gorgeous."

CHAPTER 3:
Awards and Achievements

The incredible journey and accomplishments of our favorite superstar, Taylor Swift, are absolutely amazing. In this chapter, we'll dive into all the mind-blowing awards and achievements that Taylor has earned throughout her career. From shiny golden trophies to record-breaking albums, Taylor has done it all!

Did you know that Taylor has won a whopping 14 Grammy Awards? That's right, she's taken home the music industry's biggest prize not once, not twice, but FOURTEEN times! And that's just the beginning of her award collection.

But it's not just about the awards for Taylor. She's also achieved some seriously impressive milestones that have made history in music. Like the time she became the first female artist to have three albums sell over one million copies in their first week of release. Talk about girl power!

And let's remember all the times Taylor has used her platform to make a difference in the world. From standing up for artists' rights to supporting important causes, Taylor has proven that she's not just a talented musician but also a true role model.

So, get ready to be inspired, Swifties! In this chapter, we'll focus on all the incredible ways Taylor has made her mark on the world and left us all in awe of her talent, dedication, and heart. Let's celebrate the one and only Taylor Swift together! These 13 questions celebrate her inspirational accomplishments.

1. Which award did Taylor Swift win for her album *Fearless* in 2010?

2. Which award did Taylor Swift win at the 2019 American Music Awards?

3. How many American Music Awards has she won in total?

4. Which music video of Taylor Swift's won the Video of the Year award at the 2015 MTV Video Music Awards?

5. In 2009, Taylor Swift became the youngest artist to win the Country Music Association Award for Entertainer of the Year. How old was she at the time?

6. Which song earned Taylor Swift her first Grammy Award for Best Country Song in 2012?

7. At the 2016 Grammys, Taylor Swift won the Album of the Year award for which album?

8. Which award show did Taylor Swift win eight awards at in 2013, breaking the record for the most wins by a female artist in a single night?

9. At the 2020 Sundance Film Festival, Taylor Swift won the Best Director award for her documentary. What is the name of the documentary?

10. Which album by Taylor Swift won the Grammy Award for Best Pop Vocal Album in 2010?

    a. *Taylor Swift.*

    b. *Fearless.*

    c. *Speak Now.*

    d. *Red.*

11. In 2019, Taylor Swift was named Billboard's Woman of the Decade. Which other female artist has received this honor?

    a. Beyoncé.

    b. Adele.

    c. Rihanna.

    d. Lady Gaga.

12. True or False: Taylor Swift holds the Guinness World Record for the most No. 1 hits on Billboard's US Digital Song Sales chart.

13. True or False: At the 2022 MTV Video Music Awards, Taylor Swift announced her upcoming album while accepting the award for Video of the Year.

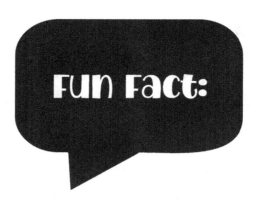

FUN FACT:

Did you know that Taylor Swift is the youngest artist ever to win the Grammy Award for Album of the Year?

Back in 2010, when Taylor was just 20 years old, she won the coveted award for her second studio album, *Fearless*. This incredible achievement made her the youngest solo artist to take home the top prize at the Grammys!

But that's not all — Taylor went on to win the Album of the Year award again in 2016 for her album *1989*, and once more in 2021 for her surprise indie-folk album *Folklore,* and again in 2024 for *Midnights*. This makes her the first and only artist to win the award four times!

So, the next time you listen to one of Taylor's award-winning albums, remember the incredible journey she's been on and the history she's made along the way. She's not just a superstar — she's a true legend!

CHAPTER 3 ANSWERS

1. Answer: Grammy Award for Album of the Year.

2. Answer: Taylor Swift won the Artist of the Decade Award.

3. Answer: 40 American Music Awards.

4. Answer: "Bad Blood" featuring Kendrick Lamar.

5. Answer: 19 years old.

6. Answer: "Mean."

7. Answer: *1989.*

8. Answer: Billboard Music Awards.

9. Answer: *Miss Americana.*

10. Answer: *Fearless.*

11. Answer: Beyoncé.

12. Answer: True, Taylor broke the record, per Guinness World Records, with 26 hits, including recent releases like "All Too Well (Taylor's Version)" and "Question...?" as well as classics like "Mine" and "Bad Blood."

13. Answer: True.

CHAPTER 4:
Tours and Performances

Are you ready to take a wild ride through the incredible world of Taylor Swift's tours and performances?

Picture this: the lights dim, the crowd goes wild, and suddenly, Taylor appears on stage in all her shimmering, sequined glory! It's a moment you'll never forget, one that Taylor has been creating for her fans for over a decade.

In this chapter, we'll explore the magic of Taylor Swift's live shows. But it's not just about the music—it's about the whole experience. The elaborate sets, the dazzling costumes, the jaw-dropping choreography—every element of a Taylor Swift show is designed to transport you to another world.

And let's not forget about the surprises! Whether she brings out special guests, plays fan-favorite songs, or unveils brand-new tracks, Taylor always has something up her sleeve to keep her Swifties on their toes.

So, get ready to test your knowledge of some of the most unforgettable moments from Taylor's tours and performances.

From the *Fearless* era to the *Reputation* stadium tour to her epic Eras tour, only true Swifties will know these questions and answers.

Are you ready, Swifties? Let's hit the stage and make some magic together! And answer these questions!

1. What was the name of Taylor Swift's first headlining tour?

2. During which tour did Taylor Swift perform a duet with Justin Timberlake?

3. Which special guest surprised fans by appearing at Taylor Swift's *Reputation* tour stop in London?

4. In which city did Taylor Swift kick off her *Red* tour?

5. Which song did Taylor Swift perform with Selena Gomez during the *Reputation* stadium tour?

6. Which tour featured a giant cobra named Karyn?

7. True or False: Taylor Swift wears a custom-made, crystal-encrusted bodysuit during her "Look What You Made Me Do" performance on the Eras Tour.

8. True or False: Taylor Swift's *Speak Now* tour visited four continents.

9. Which of the following songs did Taylor Swift perform for the first time live during the Eras Tour?
   a. "Cruel Summer."
   b. "Delicate."
   c. "All Too Well (10 Minute Version)."
   d. "The Man."

10. The *Fearless* Tour featured a special guest appearance by which country music legend?

    a. Garth Brooks.

    b. Tim McGraw.

    c. Faith Hill.

    d. Shania Twain.

11. Which of the following tours featured a surprise appearance by Lisa Kudrow, performing "Smelly Cat" from the TV show "Friends"?

    a. The *Red* Tour.

    b. The *1989* World Tour.

    c. The *Reputation* Stadium Tour.

    d. The Eras Tour.

12. On the *Fearless Tour*, Taylor Swift performed a cover of which song by The Dixie Chicks?

    a. "Wide Open Spaces."

    b. "Cowboy Take Me Away."

    c. "Goodbye Earl."

    d. "Landslide."

13. Which of the following songs has Taylor Swift performed live the most times?

    a. "Love Story"

    b. "Shake It Off"

    c. "You Belong With Me"

    d. "All Too Well."

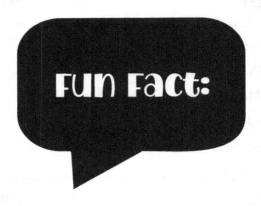

FUN FACT:

Did you know that during the *1989* World Tour, Taylor Swift invited a famous celebrity guest to join her on stage at each show?

Throughout the tour from May to December 2015, Taylor surprised her fans by bringing out a special guest at every concert. These guests included some of the biggest names in music, film, and television, such as:

✦ Justin Timberlake

✦ Selena Gomez

✦ Ellen DeGeneres

✦ Mick Jagger

✦ Kobe Bryant

✦ Cara Delevingne

✦ Alanis Morissette

✦ Idina Menzel

✦ Keith Urban

✦ Wiz Khalifa

And many more! Taylor brought out over 50 celebrity guests across the 85 shows of the *1989* World Tour. These surprise appearances delighted fans and showcased Taylor's incredible ability to connect with her fellow artists and create unforgettable moments on stage. The star-studded lineup of guests became one of the most talked-about aspects of the tour and helped to make it one of the highest-grossing tours of 2015.

The *1989* World Tour's rotating roster of celebrity guests is just one example of how Taylor Swift goes above and beyond to create unique and memorable experiences for her fans at every live show. It's no wonder her concerts are some of the most anticipated events in the music world!

Fun Fact:

Get ready to shake things up, Swifties, because this fun fact will surely blow your mind!

During Taylor Swift's Eras Tour stop in Seattle, Washington, fans literally caused the earth to move with their excitement! According to seismologist Jackie Caplan-Auerbach from Western Washington University, Swifties's enthusiastic jumping and dancing at Taylor's second Seattle show on July 23, 2023, registered as a 2.3 magnitude earthquake on local seismic stations.

Now, you might be thinking, "How is that possible?" Well, picture this: tens of thousands of fans, all jumping and dancing in unison to Taylor's iconic hits. The sheer energy and synchronization of their movements created what seismologists call a "footquake," which is a seismic event caused by human activity.

Even more incredible, this seismic activity was unique to the second night of Taylor's Seattle shows. The only difference between the two nights was that the second show started a bit later and featured two surprise songs: "Message in a Bottle" and "Tied Together with a Smile." These unexpected treats sent the crowd into an extra frenzy, causing the ground to shake with their excitement.

This fun fact is a testament to the incredible power and passion of Taylor Swift's fan base. Swifties are known for their deep connection to Taylor's music and their ability to create unforgettable moments at her live shows. But actually causing an actual earthquake? That's next-level dedication.

So, the next time someone asks you, "What's the big deal about Taylor Swift concerts?" you can tell them that Swifties don't just rock the house — they rock the whole dang planet.

Talk about making an impact!

CHAPTER 4 ANSWERS

1. Answer: The *Fearless* Tour.

2. Answer: The *1989* World Tour.

3. Answer: Niall Horan.

4. Answer: Omaha, Nebraska.

5. Answer: "Hands to Myself."

6. Answer: The *Reputation* Stadium Tour.

7. Answer: True.

8. Answer: True.

9. Answer: "Cruel Summer."

10. Answer: Tim McGraw.

11. Answer: The *1989* World Tour.

12. Answer: "Goodbye Earl."

13. Answer: "Love Story."

CHAPTER 5:
Personal Life

We all know that Taylor is an incredible musician and a fascinating person with a life full of love, friendships, and a few headline-making romances. In this chapter, we'll see how much you know about the people and relationships that have shaped Taylor's journey and inspired some of her most iconic songs.

From her early days as a rising star to her current status as a global superstar, Taylor's personal life has always been a hot topic among fans and the media. But what do we really know about the people she's dated, the friendships she's formed, and the experiences that have made her who she is today?

In this chapter, we'll test your knowledge with fun trivia questions and fascinating facts about Taylor's personal life and relationships. Get ready to learn about her famous exes, her squad of celebrity BFFs, and the stories behind some of her most personal songs.

Whether you're a die-hard fan who knows every detail of Taylor's life or a casual listener curious to learn more, this chapter has something for everyone. So, grab your friends, put on your favorite Taylor Swift album, and get ready to explore the fascinating world of her personal life and relationships.

1. Who is Taylor Swift's childhood best friend who appeared in the "Picture to Burn" music video?

2. Which famous singer is known as one of Taylor Swift's good friends and collaborators?

3. Who was Taylor Swift's date to the 2008 CMT Music Awards?

4. Who is the subject of Taylor Swift's song "Hey Stephen?"

5. Which actor did Taylor Swift date in 2009?

6. Which of Taylor Swift's celebrity friends appeared in the "Bad Blood" music video?

7. Who was Taylor Swift's date to the 2016 Met Gala?

8. Which famous couple are considered two of Taylor Swift's closest friends?

9. Which famous model is part of Taylor Swift's squad?

10. True or False: Taylor Swift's *Folklore* collaborator, Bon Iver's Justin Vernon, is also a close friend and has performed live with her on several occasions.

11. True or False: Taylor Swift's younger brother, Austin Swift, has appeared in several of her music videos, including "Christmas Tree Farm" and "The Best Day."

12. Which famous singer did Taylor Swift go on a road trip with in 2016, as documented on social media?

    a. Lorde.

    b. Katy Perry.

c. Demi Lovato.

d. Ariana Grande.

13. Which of these celebrities did Taylor Swift bake cookies with, as seen in a social media post?

a. Martha Hunt.

b. Lily Aldridge.

c. Abigail Anderson Lucier.

d. Gigi Hadid.

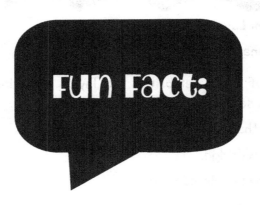

FUN FACT:

Did you know that Taylor Swift and Emma Stone have been friends since before either became famous?

Taylor and Emma first met at a mutual friend's house party in 2008, when they were both relatively unknown in their respective fields. They hit it off immediately and bonded over their shared experiences as young women trying to make it in the entertainment industry.

In the years since, Taylor and Emma have remained close friends, supporting each other through the ups and downs of their careers and personal lives. They've been spotted attending events together, like the Met Gala and the Golden Globes, and have even gone on vacation together.

In a 2015 interview with Glamour, Emma spoke about her friendship with Taylor, saying, "We've been friends for a really long time. We're very different in a lot of ways, but we're also very similar in a lot of ways. We're both really loyal and honest with each other and very emotional and sensitive."

This long-lasting friendship between Taylor and Emma is a testament to the power of female friendships and the importance of supporting and uplifting each other in a competitive and often challenging industry. It's a reminder that true friends are there for you through thick and thin, no matter how much fame or success you achieve.

So, the next time you see a photo of Taylor Swift and Emma Stone together, remember their deep and enduring friendship, which they've shared for over a decade, and the love and support they continue to offer each other to this day!

CHAPTER 5 ANSWERS

1. Answer: Abigail Anderson.

2. Answer: Ed Sheeran.

3. Answer: Joe Jonas.

4. Answer: Stephen Barker Liles (of the band Love and Theft).

5. Answer: Taylor Lautner.

6. Answer: Kendrick Lamar, Selena Gomez, Gigi Hadid, and many more.

7. Answer: Tom Hiddleston.

8. Answer: Blake Lively and Ryan Reynolds.

9. Answer: Karlie Kloss.

10. Answer: True.

11. Answer: True.

12. Answer: Lorde.

13. Answer: Abigail Anderson Lucier.

CHAPTER 6:
Taylor's Furry Friends

Attention all Swifties and animal lovers! Get ready to dive into the purr-fect world of Taylor Swift's furry friends and her unwavering love for all things cute and cuddly! Taylor's passion for animals is no secret, and her adorable feline family has captured the hearts of fans worldwide. From the sassy Meredith Grey to the sweet Olivia Benson and the charming Benjamin Button, Taylor's cats have become celebrities in their own right.

But Taylor's love for animals goes beyond her own pets. Throughout her career, she has consistently used her platform to support animal welfare organizations and raise awareness about important issues affecting our furry friends. Whether she's making generous donations to animal shelters or advocating for pet adoption, Taylor has proven time and time again that she is a true champion for animals.

Now, get ready to test your knowledge of Taylor Swift's pet posse and her animal-loving adventures! This chapter has a meow-nificent collection of trivia questions that will challenge even the most devoted Swifties. From the names of her beloved cats to their special appearances in her music videos and beyond, we've got all the details you need to become a certified expert on Taylor's furry friends. So, sharpen your claws and get ready to pounce on some paw-some trivia.

1. What are the names of Taylor Swift's three cats?

2. What is the breed of Taylor's cat, Olivia Benson?

3. In which music video does Taylor's cat, Meredith Grey, make a cameo appearance?

4. What is the name of the cat that Taylor adopted while on the set of her music video for "Me!"?

5. Which of Taylor's cats has a reputation for being the "queen" of the household?

6. What is the name of Taylor Swift's Ragdoll cat?

7. Which of Taylor's cats is named after a character from the TV show *Grey's Anatomy*?

8. True or False: Taylor had a pet hermit crab named Jules while growing up.

9. True or false: Taylor had two dogs named Bug and Baby growing up.

10. In 2023, Taylor made a "significant" donation to which animal charity to pay the medical bills for many cats?
    a. ASPCA.
    b. Beth's Furry Friends.
    c. Save a Stray,
    d. For the Animals.

11. What is the name of the song on Taylor Swift's *Lover* album that features a purring sound in the background?

    a. "I Forgot That You Existed."

    b. "Cruel Summe.r"

    c. "London Boy."

    d. "Cornelia Street."

12. Which Taylor Swift album features a song where she mentions going home to her cats?

    a. *1989.*"

    b. *The Tortured Poets Department.*

    c. *Lover.*

    d. *Reputation.*

13. Adorable kittens surround Taylor in a commercial for which product:

    a. Diet Coke.

    b. Doritos.

    c. Sunglasses

    d. Headphones.

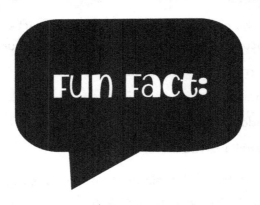

FUn FaCt:

Did you know that Taylor Swift's cat, Meredith Grey, is named after a character from the popular TV show *Grey's Anatomy*?

Taylor is a huge fan of the long-running medical drama and has often spoken about how much she loves the show and its characters. In fact, she loves it so much that she decided to name one of her beloved cats after the show's main character, Dr. Meredith Grey, played by actress Ellen Pompeo.

But the connection between Taylor's cat and the TV show doesn't end there. In 2015, Ellen Pompeo actually met her feline namesake during a visit to Taylor's apartment in New York City. The actress posted a photo of herself holding Meredith Grey on Instagram, much to the delight of fans of both the show and Taylor Swift.

Meredith Grey has since become a celebrity in her own right, frequently appearing on Taylor's social media accounts and making a cameo in one of her music videos. In the video for "Me!" featuring Brendon Urie, Meredith can be seen sitting on a couch, looking absolutely purr-fect as always.

Taylor's love for her cats and her enthusiasm for pop culture often intersect in unexpected and delightful ways, and the story behind Meredith Grey's name is just one example of how she incorporates her passions into every aspect of her life.

So, the next time you watch an episode of *Grey's Anatomy* or see a photo of Taylor Swift's adorable cat, Meredith, remember the special connection between the two and how a simple name can hold so much meaning and joy.

CHAPTER 6 ANSWERS

1. Answer: Meredith Grey, Olivia Benson, and Benjamin Button.

2. Answer: Scottish Fold.

3. Answer: "Me!" featuring Brendon Urie.

4. Answer: Benjamin Button.

5. Answer: Meredith Grey.

6. Answer: Benjamin Button.

7. Answer: Meredith Grey.

8. Answer: False.

9. Answer: True.

10. Answer: Beth's Furry Friends.

11. Answer: "Cornelia Street."

12. Answer: *Reputation* (in the song "Gorgeous").

13. Answer: A Diet Coke.

CHAPTER 7:
Philanthropy and Activism

Get ready to be inspired by the incredible heart and generosity of your favorite superstar, Taylor Swift!

In this chapter, we'll dive into the fantastic world of Taylor's philanthropy and activism. From her jaw-dropping donations to her passionate advocacy for important causes, Taylor has proven time and time again that she's not just a talented artist but also a true force for good in the world.

But here's the best part — Taylor's acts of kindness aren't just about writing big checks or making grand gestures. They're about making a real difference in the lives of individuals and communities who need it most. Whether she's surprising a sick fan with a personal concert or fighting for equality and justice, Taylor puts her whole heart into everything she does.

So, get ready to feel all the feels as we explore some of the most heartwarming and impactful moments in Taylor's philanthropic journey with some fun trivia questions. Trust us; you'll be blown away by just how much love and light this incredible woman brings into the world!

Are you ready to be inspired, Swifties? Let's dive in and discover the true magic of Taylor Swift's generous spirit!

1. What organization did Taylor Swift donate $4 million to in 2018 to support education and the arts?

2. In 2020, Taylor Swift donated $1 million to which relief fund to support those affected by the Tennessee tornadoes?

3. Which political candidate did Taylor Swift publicly endorse in the 2018 midterm elections, breaking her long-standing political silence?

4. In 2015, Taylor Swift donated all the proceeds from her single "Welcome to New York" to which city's public schools?

5. Which organization dedicated to preventing sexual assault did Taylor Swift pledge to support during her 2017 sexual assault trial?

6. Taylor Swift gives large amounts of money to what type of organizations in the communities that her Eras tour visits?

7. What organization did Talor Swift donate the proceeds from her "Wildest Dreams" music video to?

8. In 2018, Taylor Swift made a sizeable donation to the March For Our Lives campaign, which advocates for what cause?

9. True or False: In 2019, Taylor Swift donated $113,000 to the Tennessee Equality Project, an LGBTQ+ advocacy organization, to fight against discriminatory bills in her home state.

10. True or False: Taylor Swift endorsed President Joe Biden for President in 2020.

11. True or False: Taylor Swift has given over 55 million dollars in bonuses to the crew on her Eras tour.

12. In 2016, Taylor Swift donated $1 million to which organization following the devastating Louisiana floods?

    a. American Red Cross.

    b. Habitat for Humanity.

    c. The Salvation Army.

    d. United Way.

13. In 2019, Taylor Swift wrote an open letter to which U.S. Senator, urging them to support the Equality Act?

    a. Senator Bernie Sanders.

    b. Senator Kamala Harris.

    c. Senator Lamar Alexander.

    d. Senator Elizabeth Warren.

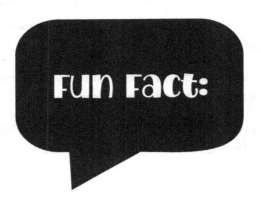

Fun Fact:

Did you know that Taylor Swift once held a private concert for a 6-year-old leukemia patient named Jordan Lee Nickerson?

In 2014, Taylor visited Boston Children's Hospital to spend time with Jordan, who was battling a rare form of leukemia. During her visit, Taylor chatted with Jordan and his family and performed an impromptu concert in his hospital room!

Sitting at Jordan's bedside, Taylor sang her hit song "We Are Never Ever Getting Back Together," complete with her signature guitar strums and Jordan's adorable sing-along moments. The heartwarming video of their duet quickly went viral, touching the hearts of millions around the world.

But Taylor's visit was more than just a viral moment — it was a testament to her genuine compassion and desire to make a difference in the lives of those facing unimaginable challenges. For Jordan and his family, Taylor's visit brought joy, laughter, and a much-needed distraction from the difficulties of battling a serious illness.

Sadly, Jordan passed away a few months after Taylor's visit, but his family expressed their gratitude for the precious memories they created together. They praised Taylor for her kindness, authenticity, and willingness to use her fame to bring happiness to others.

This fun fact showcases how Taylor Swift's philanthropy and activism often take a deeply personal and heartfelt form. By connecting with individuals like Jordan and using her talents to bring them joy, Taylor demonstrates that sometimes, the most meaningful acts of kindness are the ones that happen away from the spotlight. She is truly gift to us all!

CHAPTER 7 ANSWERS

1. Answer: The Country Music Hall of Fame and Museum.

2. Answer: Tennessee Emergency Response Fund at the Community Foundation of Middle Tennessee.

3. Answer: Phil Bredesen (Democratic candidate for U.S. Senate in Tennessee).

4. Answer: New York City.

5. Answer: Joyful Heart Foundation.

6. Answer: Food Banks.

7. Answer: African Parks Foundation of America.

8. Answer: Gun control and ending gun violence.

9. Answer: True.

10. Answer: True.

11. Answer: True.

12. Answer: American Red Cross.

13. Answer: Senator Lamar Alexander.

CHAPTER 8:
Style and Fashion

Hey there, Swifties! Get ready to dive into the fabulous and fashionable world of Taylor Swift!

When it comes to style, Taylor is in a league of her own. From her early days as a country cutie to her current status as a pop icon, she's always known how to make a statement on stage and off.

But Taylor's fashion sense isn't just about looking good - it's about expressing herself and having fun with her clothes. She's not afraid to take risks, try new things, and let her personality shine through in every outfit.

In this chapter, we'll test your knowledge of Taylor's fashion with some super fun trivia questions! From her iconic red carpet looks to her on-stage costumes and everything in between, we'll cover all the must-know details about Taylor's style evolution.

But don't worry - you don't have to be a fashion expert to join the fun! These questions are designed for Swifties of all ages and style-savvy levels. Whether you're a casual fan or a die-hard fashionista, you'll find something to love in this chapter.

So, are you ready to prove your Taylor Swift style smarts? Grab your favorite sparkly dress, put on some red lipstick, and let's get started!

1. What famous designer made Taylor Swift's dress for the 2014 Met Gala?

2. How many times has Taylor Swift been on the cover of American Vogue?

3. Which iconic fashion accessory did Taylor Swift often pair with her signature red lipstick during her *Red* era?

4. Which luxury fashion brand created the dazzling crystal-encrusted bodysuit Taylor Swift wore during her performance of "Karma" on "The Eras Tour"?

5. How many pairs of shoes were made for Taylor Swift's Eras tour?

6. True or False: Taylor Swift partnered with Keds for a sneaker line?

7. True or False: Taylor Swift's iconic "Shake It Off" music video features her wearing various costumes, including a cheerleader outfit and a ballerina dress.

8. True or False: When people attend Taylor's concerts, it is an "unofficial rule" that they dress in a way that honors Taylor's many looks over the years.

9. What color is Taylor's signature lipstick?
   a. Pink.
   b. Coral.
   c. Red.
   d. Black.

10. In the music video for "You Belong With Me," Taylor Swift wears a pretty dress to a school dance. What color is the dress?

    a. Pink.

    b. Purple.

    c. White.

    d. Black.

11. In the music video for "Me!" Taylor Swift wears a colorful dress with a particular pattern on it. What is the pattern?

    a. Polka dots.

    b. Stripes.

    c. Hearts.

    d. Flowers.

12. One of Taylor's signature looks is a black fedora hat, a white T-shirt that says "Not A Lot Going on at the Moment," black sequin shorts, and what style sunglasses?

    a. Red heart-shaped.

    b. Gold square shaped.

    c. Clear round shaped.

    d. Blue Diamond shaped.

13. What fashion accessory has Taylor made famous and is commonly traded at her concerts?

    a. Paperclip necklaces.

    b. Friendship bracelets.

    c. Fingerless gloves.

    d. Cowboy hats.

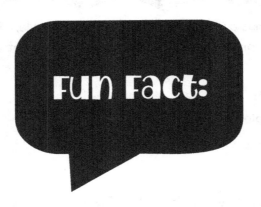

Fun Fact:

Taylor Swift is known for her impeccable attention to detail regarding her fashion choices, including her nail polish. She often chooses colors that perfectly match or complement the colors in her clothing, creating a cohesive and polished look from head to toe.

For example, at the 2014 Met Gala, Taylor wore a stunning pink gown with a long train. To complete the look, she chose a soft pink nail polish that matched the color of her dress perfectly. It was a small but significant detail that showed how much thought and care she put into every aspect of her appearance.

At other events, Taylor has been spotted with nail polish colors that contrast with her outfits in a fun and eye-catching way. For example, she might wear a bright red dress with pale blue nail polish or a black-and-white outfit with a pop of neon yellow on her nails. These unexpected color combinations show off her creativity and playful side.

Taylor's love for matching her nails to her outfits is an excellent example of how even minor details can impact fashion. It's a fun way to express yourself and add an extra touch of personality to your look. Taylor's attention to detail and love for matching her nails to her outfits are just one of the many ways she shows her passion for fashion.

CHAPTER 8 ANSWERS

1. Answer: Oscar de la Renta.

2. Answer: 4.

3. Answer: A black fedora hat.

4. Answer: Roberto Cavalli.

5. Answer: 250.

6. Answer: True.

7. Answer: True.

8. Answer: True.

9. Answer: Red.

10. Answer: White.

11. Answer: Polka dots.

12. Answer: Red heart-shaped.

13. Answer: Friendship bracelets.

CHAPTER 9:
Collaborations and Friendships

Get ready to dive into the incredible world of Taylor Swift's collaborations and musical friendships!

Throughout her career, Taylor has worked with some of the biggest names in music, creating unforgettable songs and iconic moments that have left us all in awe. From her early days as a country sweetheart to her current status as a pop superstar, Taylor has always had a knack for attracting the most talented artists and creating magic both in the studio and on stage.

But Taylor's collaborations aren't just about making great music but also about building lasting friendships and supporting each other's creative journeys. Whether co-writing with her bestie Ed Sheeran or performing on stage with her idol Keith Urban, Taylor puts her heart and soul into every collaboration she takes on.

In this chapter, we'll test your knowledge of Taylor's most memorable collaborations and their stories. From the chart-topping hits to the hidden gems, we've got a whole bunch of trivia questions that will challenge even the most die-hard Swifties.

1. Which singer-songwriter has Taylor Swift collaborated with on multiple songs, including "Everything Has Changed" and "End Game?"

2. Taylor Swift and which pop star famously ended their feud and reconciled in the music video for "You Need to Calm Down?"

3. Which country music duo did Taylor Swift collaborate with on the song "Highway Don't Care?"

4. Taylor Swift and which actress have been close friends since meeting at the 2008 MTV Video Music Awards?

5. Taylor Swift and which actress played on-screen best friends in the movie *Valentine's Day*?

6. Which pop star did Taylor Swift collaborate with on the remix of her song "Lover?"

7. Taylor Swift and which country music singer co-wrote the song "Best Days of Your Life" from Swift's album *Fearless*?

8. True or False: Taylor Swift and Beyoncé have collaborated on a song together?

9. True or False: Taylor Swift collaborated with Kendrick Lamar on the song "Bad Blood" from her album *1989*.

10. True or False: Taylor Swift co-wrote the song "This Is What You Came For" with Calvin Harris, which Rihanna performed.

11. Who collaborated with Taylor Swift on the song "Safe & Sound" for *The Hunger Games* soundtrack?

    a. The Civil Wars.

    b. The Chicks (formerly Dixie Chicks.)

    c. Mumford & Sons.

    d. The Lumineers.

12. Which artist collaborated with Taylor Swift on the song "Everything Has Changed" from her album *Red*?

    a. Ed Sheeran.

    b. Bon Iver.

    c. Brendon Urie.

    d. Gary Lightbody.

13. Which artist was featured on the remix of Taylor Swift's song "Willow" from her album *Evermore*?

    a. Bon Iver.

    b. Haim.

    c. The National.

    d. Phoebe Bridgers.

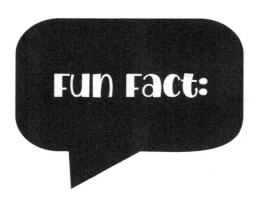

Fun Fact:

Did you know that Taylor Swift and Ed Sheeran have matching tattoos?

Taylor and Ed have been close friends and collaborators for years, having worked together on songs like "Everything Has Changed" and "End Game." But their connection goes beyond making music together—they also share a special bond through their matching tattoos!

In 2012, while Taylor was on tour with Ed as her opening act, the two got matching tattoos to commemorate their friendship and the success of their collaboration on "Everything Has Changed." They chose a simple yet meaningful design—a small red tattoo inspired by the title of Taylor's album at the time.

The tattoo session took place backstage after one of their shows. Ed tattooed the word red onto Taylor's arm, and Taylor returned the favor by inking the same word onto Ed's arm. It was a spontaneous and fun moment that showcased their playful and affectionate relationship.

Since then, the two have continued to collaborate and support each other's careers, with Ed appearing as a surprise guest at several of Taylor's concerts. Their matching tattoos are a permanent reminder of their creative partnership and their special bond.

CHAPTER 9 ANSWERS

1. Answer: Ed Sheeran.

2. Answer: Katy Perry.

3. Answer: Tim McGraw and Keith Urban.

4. Answer: Selena Gomez.

5. Answer: Emma Stone.

6. Answer: Shawn Mendes.

7. Answer: Kellie Pickler.

8. Answer: False.

9. Answer: True.

10. Answer: True.

11. Answer: The Civil Wars.

12. Answer: Ed Sheeran.

13. Answer: Haim.

CHAPTER 10:
Easter Eggs and Hidden Meaning

Hey there, Swifties! Are you ready to dive into the mysterious and enchanting world of Taylor Swift's Easter eggs and hidden meanings?

We all know no one loves communicating in secret, subtle ways more than Taylor! She loves to drop hints and give clues to upcoming songs, albums, meaning in her lyrics, and more! She is an absolute master at this, and part of what makes us love her so much. She is the queen of clever wordplay, sneaky references, and secret messages, sprinkling them throughout her music and videos. It's like a treasure hunt for her most dedicated fans, and these questions are designed to test your detective skills.

This chapter is a collection of brain-teasing trivia questions that will challenge your knowledge of Taylor's most iconic Easter eggs and hidden meanings. We've covered everything from the symbolic imagery in her music videos to the cryptic lyrics hinting at her personal life.

But don't worry, you don't need to be a master detective to enjoy this chapter. Whether you're a die-hard Swiftie or a casual fan, you'll find plenty of fascinating facts and aha moments that will make you appreciate Taylor's artistry even more.

So, put on your thinking cap, grab your magnifying glass, and get ready to unravel the mysteries of Taylor Swift's musical universe. Who knows, you might even discover a new hidden message that nobody else has noticed before!

Are you up for the challenge, Swifties? Let's see how many Easter eggs you can crack and how many secret meanings you can uncover. Get ready for a wild ride through the rabbit hole of Taylor's imagination. The Easter egg hunt starts now!

1. Which family member's name appears on the Marquee in Taylor's "Wildest Dreams" video?

2. There are two Easter eggs in Taylor's "Cardigan" Music video; what are they?

3. In the music video for "You Need to Calm Down," Ellen Degeneres gets a tattoo that is an Easter egg. What does the tattoo say?

4. In the music video for "The Man," what does the sign no scooter sign hint at?

5. In the video for "Look What You Made Me Do," Taylor is sitting on a throne, wearing snake rings, and being served tea by two snakes next to candles held up by elaborate snake candelabras. What are these snakes referencing?

6. True or False: In the "Look What You Made Me Do" music video, Taylor Swift's character wears a shirt reminiscent of the T-shirt she wore in her "You Belong to Me" video. On

the new shirt, Taylor has written the names of some of her real-life best friends.

7. True or False: In the "ME!" music video, Taylor Swift is seen wearing a pin that says "Lover," hinting at the title of her upcoming album.

8. True or False: In Taylor's "Style" video, she is seen tearing a paper airplane necklace from her neck. Who does this necklace reference?

9. Taylor left hidden messages in her CD liners for her fans by:
   a. Drawing cute pictures.
   b. Color-coding words to match her albums.
   c. Capitalizing certain letters to reveal a message.
   d. Inserting QR codes.

10. In the "Karma" music video, Taylor stands on a pedestal with a hidden message. What does the message say?
    a. Red.
    b. 1989.
    c. Lover.
    d. Taylor Swift.

11. The *All Too Well the Short Film* features a 1989 Mercedes; this is a reference to:
    a. Taylor's love of Mercedes.
    b. Taylor's birth year.
    c. Taylor's love of cars.
    d. The name of an upcoming song.

12. Koi Fish are featured in Taylor's "Lavender Haze" video, hinting at which album might be the next for Taylor to release:

    a. *Speak Now.*

    b. *Taylor Swift.*

    c. *Evermore.*

    d. *Red.*

13. Taylor's zodiac sign and her then-boyfriend's, Joe Alwyn's, zodiac signs are seen together in which music video?

    a. "End Game."

    b. "Shake it Off."

    c. "Lavender Haze."

    d. "Love Story."

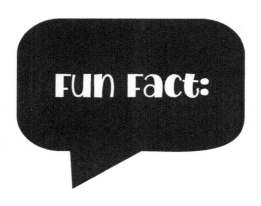

FUN FACT:

One well-known example of an Easter egg in Taylor Swift's lyrics can be found in her song "Gorgeous" from the album *Reputation*. In the song's opening lines, a baby voice says, "Gorgeous."

Many fans speculated about the identity of the mysterious baby voice, with guesses ranging from Taylor's own niece to a random sound effect. However, it was later revealed that the voice actually belongs to James Reynolds, the daughter of Blake Lively and Ryan Reynolds, who are close friends with Taylor.

This hidden detail was a clever way for Taylor to incorporate a personal touch into the song while also leaving a fun little mystery for her fans to unravel. It demonstrates her playful approach to songwriting and her love for planting Easter eggs that reward her most attentive and dedicated listeners.

By including a snippet of James Reynolds' voice, Taylor gave a subtle shout-out to her celebrity pals and added an extra layer of meaning and intrigue to the song. It's a prime example of how she uses seemingly random or innocuous details to create deeper connections and narratives within her music.

CHAPTER 10 ANSWERS

1. Answer: Her grandmother, Marjorie Finlay.

2. Answer: The analog clock is set to 1:15, the hands are on the 1 and the 3, which is a hidden reference to 13, and the picture of the man in the frame is Taylor's grandfather!!!

3. Answer: Cruel Summer.

4. Answer: Taylor's feud with Scooter Braun, who bought the rights to her Master's.

5. Answer: Her feud with Kim Kardashian and Kanye West.

6. Answer: True.

7. Answer: False.

8. Answer: Harry Styles.

9. Answer: Capitalizing certain letters to reveal a message.

10. Answer: 1989.

11. Answer: Taylor's birth year; it is a **1989** Mercedes-Benz.

12. Answer: *Speak Now*.

13. Answer: "Lavender Haze."

CHAPTER 11:
Swifties

Hey there, Swifties! Are you ready to dive into the wonderful, wacky, and wildly passionate world of Taylor Swift's fan community? Welcome to the chapter all about YOU!

If you're a Swiftie, you already know that being a fan of Taylor Swift is so much more than just listening to her music. It's a way of life, a community, and a shared love that connects people from all around the world. Swifties are known for their incredible dedication, creativity, and unwavering support for Taylor and each other.

In this chapter, the questions are dedicated to all of Taylor's amazing fans and all the amazing ways they express their love for Taylor and come together as a fandom. From decoding hidden messages in her lyrics to organizing massive online and in-person events, Swifties are always finding new and exciting ways to celebrate their idol.

But being a dedicated fan isn't just about the fun and games. It's also about fans' deep emotional connection with Taylor and her music. Many fans credit Taylor with helping them through tough times, inspiring them to be their best selves, and giving them a sense of belonging and purpose. So, whether you're a die-hard fan who knows every lyric by heart or a curious observer who wants to learn more about this fascinating fan culture, this chapter has something for everyone.

But enough talking - let's get to the good stuff! Put on your favorite Taylor Swift album, grab your Swiftie merch, and let's dive into some fun questions about the wild and wonderful world of Taylor Swift fandom.

1. What popular hashtag do Swifties use on social media to show their love for Taylor?

    a. #SwiftieNation.

    b. #TaylorSwiftFanClub.

    c. #WeAreSwifties.

    d. #SwiftieForever.

2. Which famous celebrity is known for being a major Swiftie?

    a. Selena Gomez.

    b. Emma Stone

    c. Blake Lively.

    d. All of the above.

3. What is the term used to describe Taylor Swift's fans who are known for their high levels of participation, creativity, loyalty, community, and dedication to Taylor Swift?

    a. Tay Tays.

    b. Swifties.

    c. Reds.

    d. Taylorites.

4. What is the nickname given to Taylor Swift's close circle of celebrity friends?

   a. The Swift Squad.

   b. Tay's Besties.

   c. The Swiftie Crew.

   d. Taylor's Angels.

5. Swifties often swap what item?

   a. Baking recipes.

   b. Stories about pet cats.

   c. Butterfly necklaces.

   d. Friendship bracelets.

6. What hashtag did Swifties popularize on social media to show their support during Taylor's dispute with her former label?

   a. #JusticeForTaylor.

   b. #IStandWithTaylor.

   c. #TaylorSwiftIsFree.

   d. #SupportTaylor.

7. What do Swifties often do to celebrate the release of a new Taylor Swift album?

   a. Throw parties.

   b. Organize streaming parties.

   c. Host listening sessions.

   d. All of the above.

8. True or False: Swifties are interested in Taylor Swift's music, fashion, philanthropy, and personal life.

9. True or False: Swifties often wear outfits inspired by Taylor's latest album, video, or tour.

10. True or False: Swifties have a reputation for being welcoming and inclusive to all fans, regardless of age, gender, or background.

11. True or False: Swifties frequently give to charity in Taylor Swift's name. Taylor Swift's fans are known for their generosity and community spirit, often organizing charitable initiatives inspired by Taylor's own philanthropic efforts.

12. Swifties are described as the following:
    a. Female.
    b. Male.
    c. Between the ages of 3 and 100.
    d. All of the Above.

13. What term do Swifties use to describe the process of finding hidden messages in Taylor Swift's lyrics, videos, and social media posts?

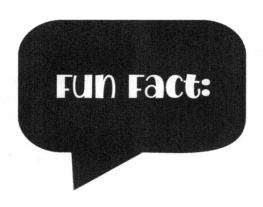

FuN FacT:

Did you know that Swifties have their own secret language and codes?

That's right, Swifties have developed a complex system of inside jokes, references, and acronyms that only true fans can understand. It's like a secret club that you can only join if you know the password (which is probably a lyric from a deep cut on one of Taylor's albums).

For example, if you see a Swiftie tweet "TIWWCHNT" or "YBWM," don't worry - they haven't lost their minds. They're referencing some of Taylor's most iconic songs, "This Is Why We Can't Have Nice Things" and "You Belong With Me." And if someone says they're feeling "13," it's not a math problem - it's a reference to Taylor's lucky number.

But Swifties' secret language goes beyond song titles and numbers. They also have their own terminology for different eras of Taylor's career, like the *Fearless* Era or the *Red* Era, and they use emojis and hashtags to convey complex emotions and ideas.

In fact, the Swiftie code is so intricate and ever-evolving that it can sometimes feel like a full-time job just to keep up with all the references and inside jokes. But for true Swifties, it's all part of the fun and excitement of being part of such a passionate and creative fan community.

So the next time you see a Swiftie tweeting what looks like gibberish, just know that they're probably communicating in their special language - which only true fans can understand. It's like having a secret handshake or a decoder ring, but instead of joining a spy agency, you're joining a worldwide community of music lovers and friends.

Pretty cool, right?

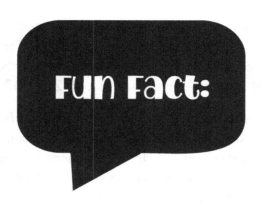

FUN FACT:

Did you know that Taylor Swift made history during her Eras Tour stop in Edinburgh, Scotland, in June of 2024?

The pop superstar performed three sold-out shows at Murrayfield Stadium, which has a whopping capacity of 67,144 people. But that's not all — Taylor didn't just sell out the stadium once, but three times in a row, breaking the all-time attendance record for a stadium show in Scotland with each performance!

An incredible 220,000 Swifties gathered to witness Taylor's epic performances in Edinburgh. That's like the entire population of a small city all coming together to celebrate their love for Taylor and her music!

To put this achievement into perspective, consider this: before Taylor, no artist had ever sold out Murrayfield Stadium three times in a row. In fact, many artists struggle to sell out even one night at a venue of that size. But leave it to Taylor not only to accomplish this feat but also to do it three times over, setting a new record with each show!

After the final Edinburgh performance, Taylor took to Instagram to express her gratitude to the fans who made this historic moment possible. In a heartfelt post, she wrote,

"Edinburgh!!! You truly blew me away this weekend. Thank you for breaking the all-time attendance record for a stadium show in Scotland 3 times in a row and for all the ways you made us feel right at home. Love you, all 220,000 of you!!!

So, there you have it — proof that Taylor Swift is not just a record-breaking artist but a force to be reckoned with. With the power to draw in hundreds of thousands of fans and make history wherever she goes, there's no doubt that she's one of the most influential and beloved musicians of our time.

CHAPTER 11 ANSWERS

1. Answer: #SwiftieNation.

2. Answer: All of the above.

3. Answer: Swifties.

4. Answer: The Swift Squad.

5. Answer: Friendship bracelets.

6. Answer: #IStandWithTaylor.

7. Answer: All of the above.

8. Answer: True.

9. Answer: True.

10. Answer: True.

11. Answer: True.

12. Answer: All of the Above.

13. Answer: Easter Egg Hunting.

Conclusion

As we end this incredible journey through Taylor Swift's life and career, it's impossible not to feel a sense of awe and inspiration at all she has accomplished. From her early days as a young girl with big dreams to her current status as one of the most influential and beloved artists of our time, Taylor has never ceased to amaze us with her talent, creativity, and unwavering commitment to her craft.

Through the 143 trivia questions and 13 fun facts in this book, we've had the chance to explore every aspect of Taylor's artistry, from her songwriting and musicianship to her fashion choices and philanthropic efforts. We've seen how she has consistently pushed boundaries, defied expectations, and used her platform to make a positive difference in the world.

But perhaps the most remarkable thing about Taylor Swift is how she has connected with her fans on such a deep and personal level. Through her music, she has given voice to millions of people's hopes, fears, and dreams worldwide, offering comfort, inspiration, and a sense of belonging to anyone who has ever felt lost or alone.

Looking back on all we've learned about Taylor through this book, it's clear that her impact on the world of music and popular culture is immeasurable. She has redefined what it means to be a star in the 21st century, and her influence will be felt for generations.

Even more than that, Taylor Swift has shown us the power of staying true to ourselves, following our dreams and using our voices to make a difference in the world. She has inspired countless young people to pick up a guitar, write a song, or stand up for what they believe in, and her legacy will continue to inspire and empower people for years to come.

So, as we close the pages of this book, let us take a moment to celebrate Taylor Swift's incredible journey and all that she represents. Let us be grateful for the music that has brought us together, the stories that have touched our hearts, and the memories that will last a lifetime.

Let us continue to support and celebrate this remarkable artist as she grows, evolves, and makes her mark on the world. If there's one thing we know for sure, the best is yet to come for Taylor Swift and her fans.

Thank you for joining us on this journey through the world of Taylor Swift. We hope this book has brought you joy, laughter, and a deeper appreciation for the magic of music and the power of one incredible artist.

Remember, keep shining bright, and never stop believing in the power of your dreams!